treehouse

ISBN: 978-0-692-63378-6

info@treehousec.com
info@feedthetoilets.org

Welcome, and thank you for your interest in *I Want To Eat Your Poo.*

If you're reading this, chances are you already give your poo to a toilet on a regular basis . But did you know there are some people, mostly small children, who selfishly choose not to feed their poo to toilets? As a result, thousands of toilets go to bed hungry every night, even in wealthy countries like the United States, where there is more than enough poo to go around.

By purchasing this book, you have taken the first step in helping to break the cycle of toilet hunger. Consider sharing copies with your friends and family. **Give a coloring book or a coffee mug to a loved one.** The more we can spread awareness of this epidemic, the more lives we can change, even if the action you take means helping just one toilet.

For more information, resources, and other products, please visit www.feedthetoilets.org. There is a hungry toilet waiting for you there.

feedthetoilets.org

I Want to Eat Your Poo

by Professor Alan Cuttlefish

Timmy was a happy boy,
A lot like you and me.
He liked to run and jump and play
And climb the tallest tree.

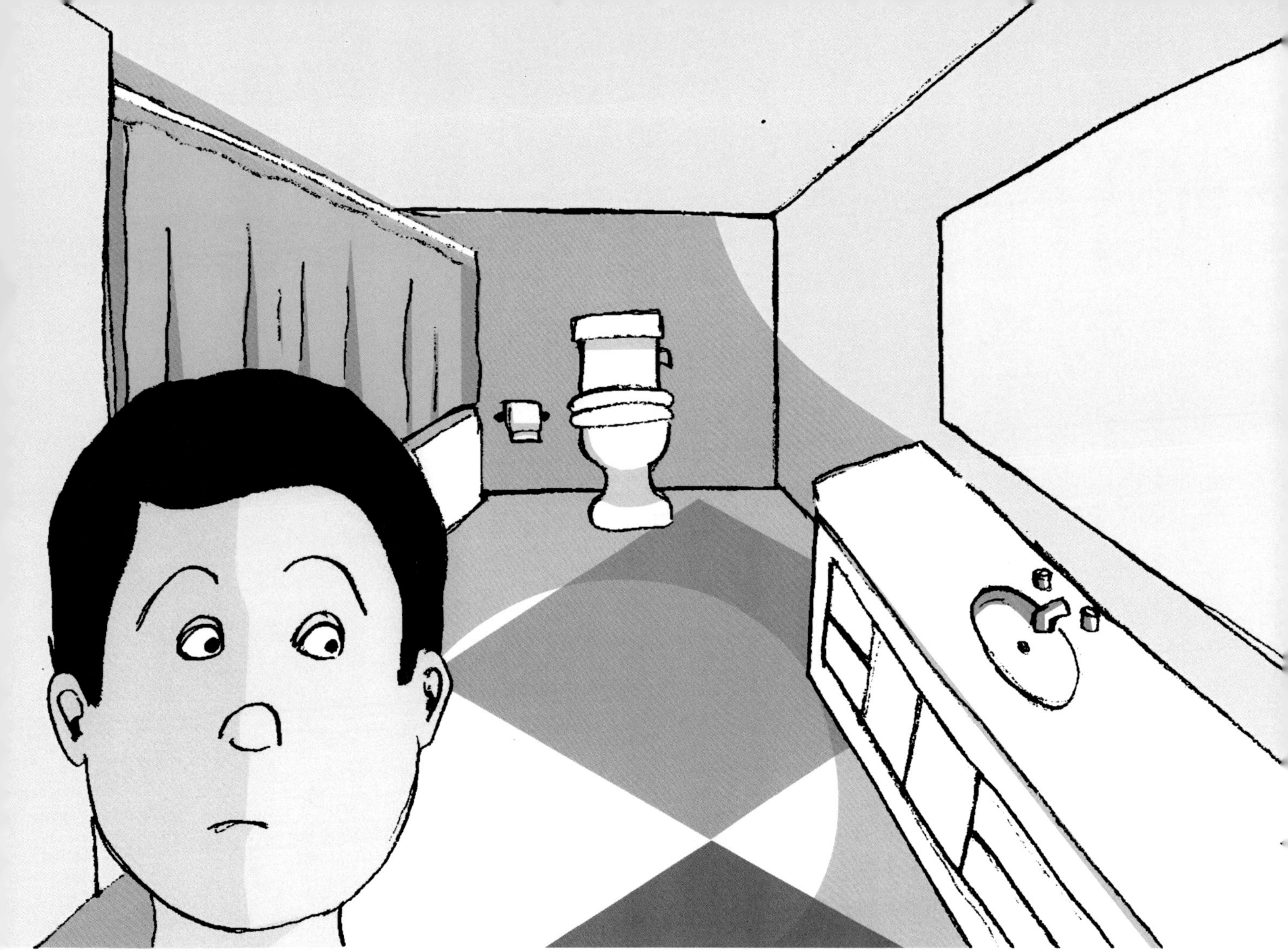

Timmy was a great big boy,
But not quite big enough.
The act of pooping in the toilet
Simply was too tough.

One night, Timmy brushed his teeth,
As he was taught to do,
When suddenly a voice called out,
"I want to eat your poo."

"What? Who said that?" Timmy asked.
"Who's there? Where are you?"
The voice repeated, clear as day,
"I want to eat your poo."

"Surely this cannot be real,"
A puzzled Timmy said.
He left the bathroom, said his prayers,
And put himself to bed.

The next day in the backyard,
His concerns reached a crescendo,
When *"I want to eat your poo..."*
Drifted from the upstairs window.

Most boys would have called for help
Or found a place to hide.
But Timmy couldn't rest
'Til this voice was identified.

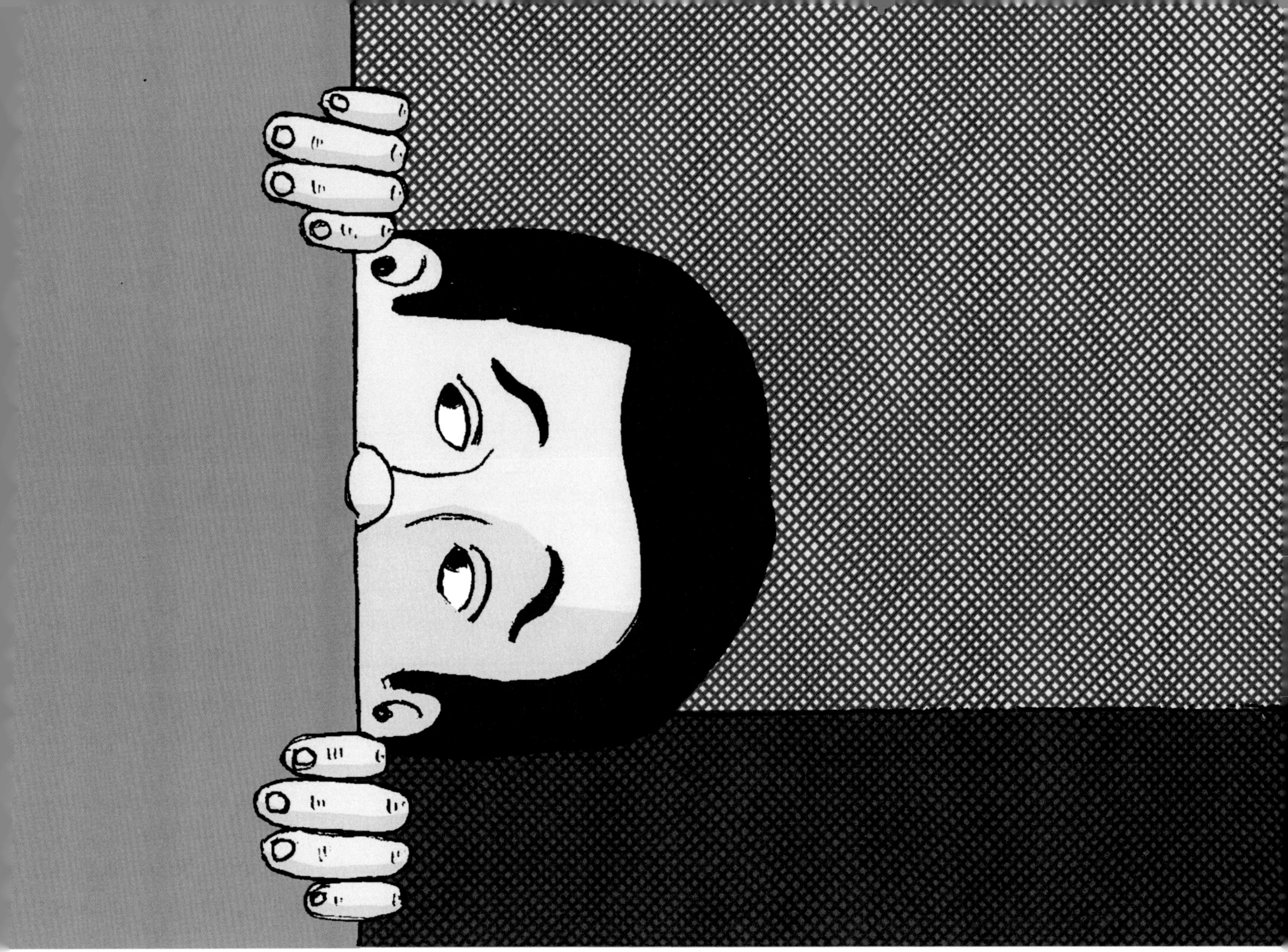

He peeked into the bathroom,
Where he had first heard the words.
"What could it be, this creepy thing
That wants to eat my turds?"

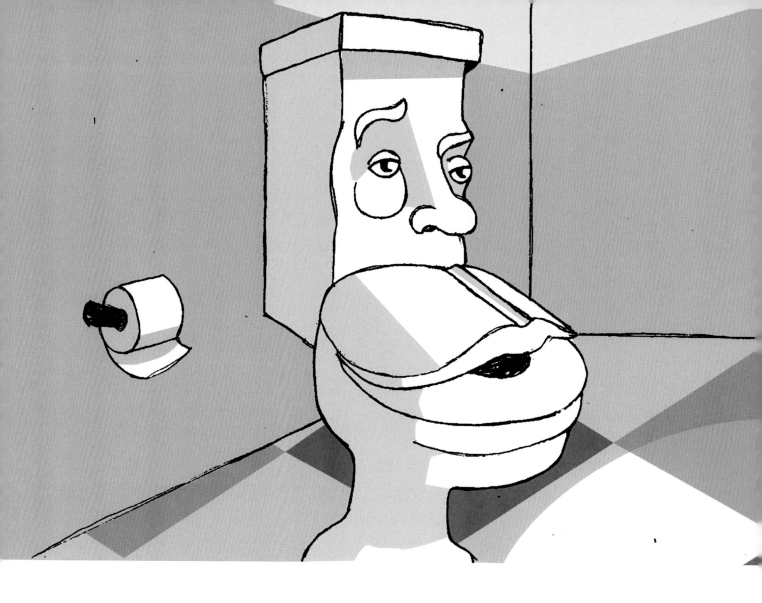

With eyebrows raised, the toilet replied,
"Creepy? That's not me.
I simply need to eat your poo
To stay alive, you see."

Timmy bellowed loudly
As he leapt into the air.
He'd never noticed eyes nor nose
Upon the potty chair.

"I'm sorry if I've startled you,
But I am very hungry.
At this point, I'd eat anything:
Lumpy, bumpy, runny."

"Why would I give you my poo
And go through all the trouble?
Every time I poo, my mother
Cleans it on the double."

"You may have many options,
Some of which are more convenient,
But to withhold from the hungry
is a choice that's downright deviant!"

"I'd better go," said Timmy.
"Mom said not to talk to strangers."
The toilet tried his best,
But he could not contain his anger.

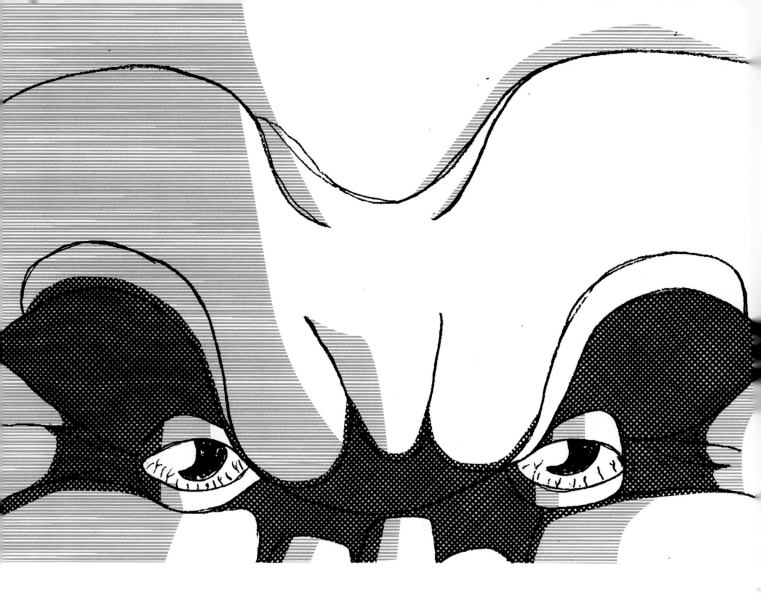

"Porcelain and water are
The only things I'm made of.
I do not understand what it is
You are so afraid of!"

Timmy shrugged and bounded off.
The toilet heaved a sigh.
He had a sinking feeling.
Without poo, he'd surely die.

Timmy went about his day
And doubted what he'd heard.
Even small boys know that
Talking toilets are absurd.

Later in the evening time,
Tucked tightly in his bed,
Timmy closed his eyes, and
Nightmares swirled around his head.

A swarm of snakes sprung from
The toilet's mouth onto the floor.
From room to room, they nipped his heels
As Timmy screamed in horror.

He tumbled down the staircase,
Where the toilet stood and caught him.
Flushed downstream, poor Timmy yelped
When something bit his bottom.

Hundreds of piranhas
Chased our Timmy through the lake.
Just as they caught up,
He shot up in his bed, awake.

In the corner of his bedroom
sat a thin and shriveled figure.
A moment passed, and then it spoke.
"I hope you'll reconsider."

The toilet moved into the moonlight,
From the shadow's veil.
With grey and sunken eyes,
He hadn't ever looked so frail.

"I hate to disappoint, but
What more can I say to you?
There's no way I'll ever
Give you any of my poo."

"There's nothing I can say or do
To make you change your mind?"
Timmy shook his head.
"I'm sorry if that seems unkind."

"Can't you see I'm starving, boy!?
It's just the thing to do!"
Timmy answered flatly,
"You will never eat my poo."

"I'm a reasonable toilet;
Very patient with beginners.
But your selfishness leaves me with
Just one way to get my dinner."

The toilet bared his teeth,
Each one much sharper than a knife.
As he came closer, Timmy begged
And bargained for his life.

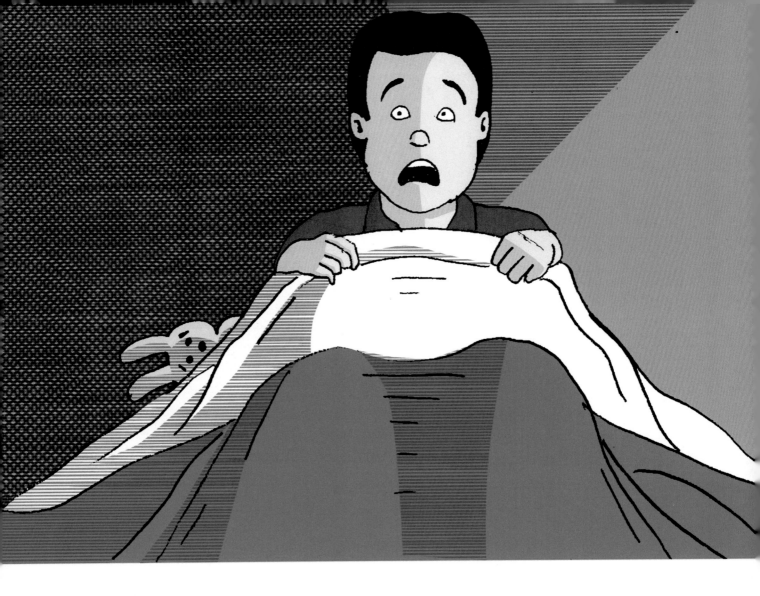

"I know lots of people,
Ten or twenty in the least,
Who go potty in the toilet
And could bring you quite a feast!"

The toilet grinned. *"I like that plan,*
A poo feast would be great.
I hope they visit soon,
But for tonight it is too late."

All of Timmy's loved ones
Miss the young man very much.
And the toilet thinks about him fondly
Every time he's flushed.

So don't take your poo for granted,
And don't keep it to yourself.
Toilets the world over
Rely on it for their health.

Hungry for more?

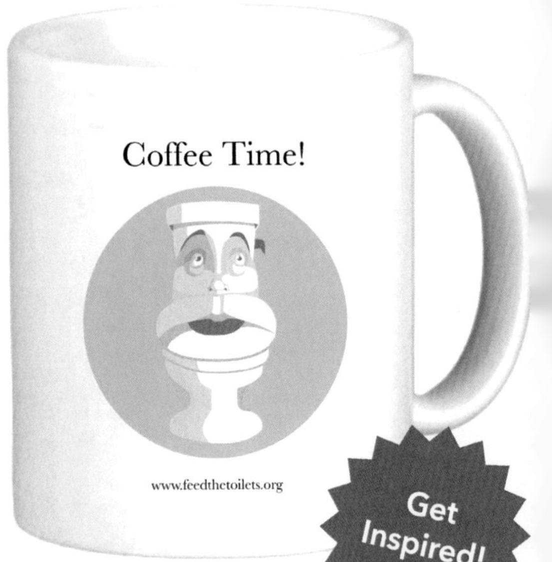
Coffee Time!
www.feedthetoilets.org

Get Inspired!

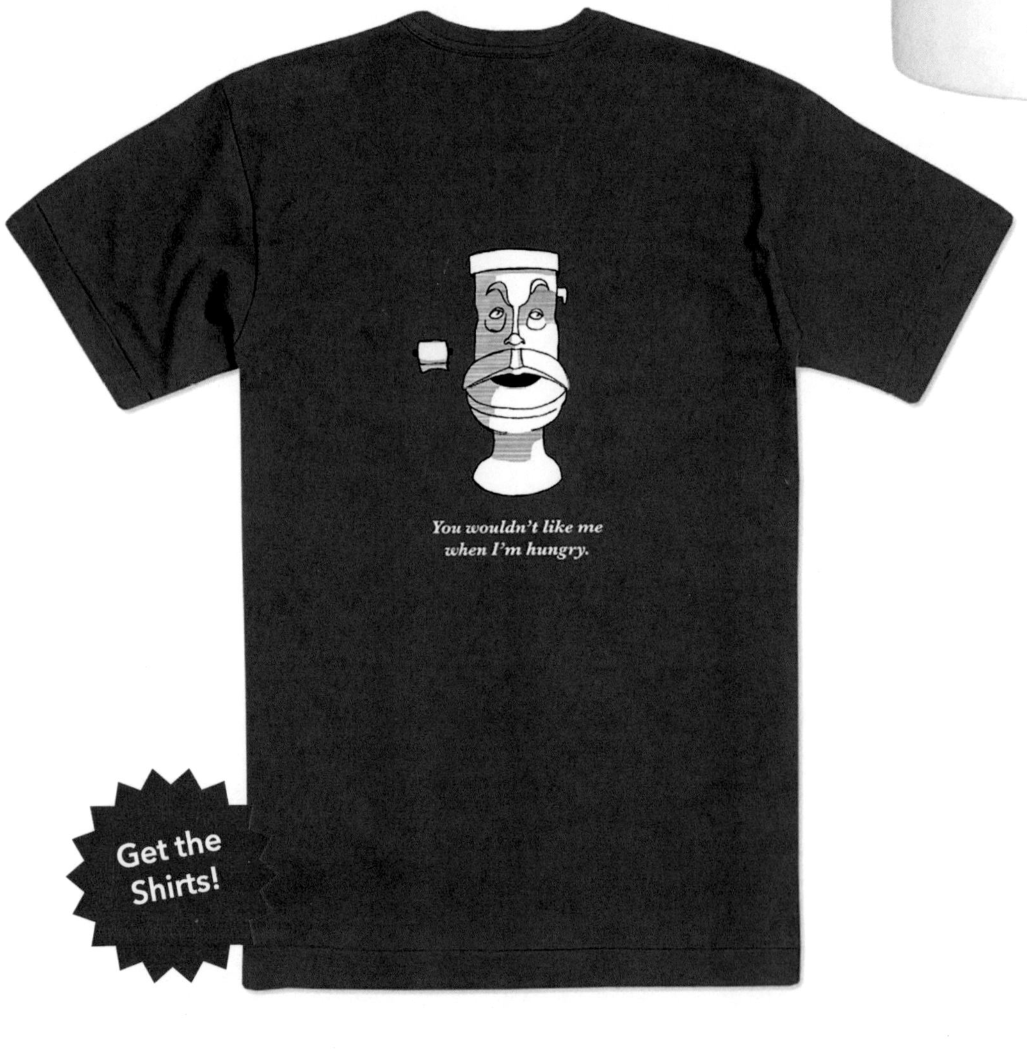
You wouldn't like me
when I'm hungry.

Get the Shirts!

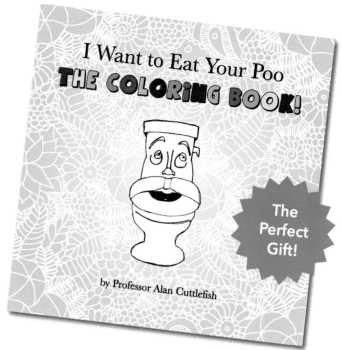

32661520R00022

Made in the USA
San Bernardino, CA
17 April 2019